THE KITTY

Who Rescued Me
After I Rescued Him

SHAWN P. FLYNN

Shiloh,
To a Fellow Kitty Lover!

ABBE ROAD PUBLISHING

ABBE ROAD PUBLISHING

Publisher's Cataloging-In-Publication Data
(Prepared by The Donohue Group, Inc.)

Names: Flynn, Shawn P., 1963-
Title: The kitty who rescued me after I rescued him / Shawn P. Flynn.
Description: First edition. | [Enfield, Connecticut] : Abbe Road
    Publishing, 2017. | Originally published: [Shawn P. Flynn], 2016.
Identifiers: LCCN 2017903489 | ISBN 978-0-9987880-0-5 (paperback) | ISBN
    978-0-9987880-1-2 (ebook)
Subjects: LCSH: Flynn, Shawn P. | Cat owners--Psychology. | Human-animal
    relationships. | Cat rescue.
Classification: LCC SF442.86 .F59 2017 (print) | LCC SF442.86 (ebook) |
    DDC 636.8--dc23

Abbe Road Publishing books may be purchased for educational, business, or
promotional use. For information on bulk purchases, please contact the
publisher at 1-203-623-7710.

Previously published as The Kitty: Who Rescued Me After I Rescued Him in
2016 ISBN 978-1539349457

DEDICATION

To Kitty, my Kitty Boy, the Kitty Lover, my Sexy Lover
Boy, the Original Kitty Lover, who rescued his daddy
after his daddy rescued him, who not only stole his
daddy's heart and turned him into a kitty lover, but
turned him into a Kitty Lover

CONTENTS

ACKNOWLEDGMENTS

Thanks to my friends Tom, MaryAnn and Stretch, and my sister Kara, who provided feedback on my initial manuscript, and thanks to my editors who pushed me to include details that were often painful to write about. But, most importantly, thanks to my girlfriend Carrie for her love and support, and encouraging me to pursue this project.

• *Chapter 1* •

MEETING KITTY

PEOPLE COME IN AND OUT of our lives every day and make little or no real impact on us. But every now and then, someone or something comes into a life and changes it forever.

I first met Kitty in April 2006, when my fiancée and I were looking at a house we were thinking of buying. It was a beautiful, sunny Sunday afternoon. The snow had all melted, and as a result, the ground was still a little soggy. We were walking in the backyard, just looking around and trying to get a feel for the property. This big, bushy orange cat with the prettiest green eyes was hanging around, and I said, "Kitty," as I am a big animal lover. He was really friendly and walked over and rubbed against my leg. I figured he was a neighbor's cat and didn't think much of it.

After looking at probably thirty houses in north-central Connecticut, we ended up buying the one in Enfield where we had met Kitty. We closed on the property on Friday, June 2, and moved in the following day. It was a rainy, miserable day, especially for June. I had to back the rental truck up as close to the garage as I could get it to try to keep the stuff we were moving from getting wet. Fortunately, my buddies Tom and Phil helped us move. The rain stopped the following day, and Monday turned out to be gorgeous. Of course, because it was Monday, that meant that I had to go to work.

I got home from work at about five thirty or six on Monday, and that same stray cat was sitting on the front step like he was waiting for me to get home. I said hi to him, gave him a pat on the head, and went inside to get a few things done.

I went to turn on the water at the kitchen sink, and lo and behold, the water was shut off. Apparently, the attorneys had gotten everything but the water switched to my name at the closing. I grabbed the phone book and started to call around to get the water turned back on. I finally called the right place, and they said they could send someone out to turn on the water; however, an emergency service call from the water company was going to cost $175, and I had to have a check ready for the service tech when he arrived. I reluctantly agreed. While I was waiting, I called my attorney and shared the situation with him. He told me to just cut the guy a check, and we would figure out who was responsible and should pay the cost the following day.

I grabbed a beer and my checkbook and went out front to sit on the stoop to wait for the water guy. The cat was still sitting on the front step. I sat down next to him and petted and talked to him as I drank my beer. I was complaining about how the water was turned off and I was going to have to pay $175 to get it turned back on.

The water-company guy pulled up a short time later. He took some kind of tool out of the back of his truck, walked over to the side of the property, used the tool to turn something in the grass, and was done. I thought, "A hundred and seventy-five bucks for that?"

He threw the tool back into his truck and walked over to collect his payment. I thanked him for coming out and reluctantly gave him the check. We were making small talk when he saw the cat lying on my front step and yelled, "Buster!"

The cat's head came whipping around like he knew the guy, who said something like, "That's my cat. He's been missing for a couple of years now."

He asked if I had adopted the cat yet, and I told him,

"No, I just moved in on Saturday." He asked me if he could have him, and I said, "He's not mine."

So he handed me back my check and said, "This is for finding my cat." He went over, picked the cat up, got in his truck, and drove off.

Three days later, when I got home from work, the cat was sitting on the front stoop again.

• *Chapter 2* •

SUMMER OF 2006

SO, THAT WAS THE SUMMER I met Kitty. While he was originally just a kitty, he quickly became *the* Kitty, because that was what I called him, and he came to know it as his name.

A few weeks after the water incident, I was driving my truck up the street and saw the same water-company guy cutting the grass in his front yard. I assumed that was where he took Kitty when he left my house. It was about three or four miles from where I lived. I still don't know if Kitty was really that guy's cat or not. My fiancée and I speculated that maybe the guy took Kitty home and his wife said, "That's not Buster. Are you on drugs? Get him outta here."

So Kitty made it back. Something drew him to our house, and he obviously felt comfortable there. According to my next-door neighbor Randy, Kitty had lived in the backyard for two or three years. The property had been vacant for at least a year before we moved in. Before that, the former owner had let his teenage and young-adult sons live there. Randy said Kitty used to sit in the grass in his backyard and watch him clean the pool. He called him Garfield.

I was never much of a cat person, but only because I didn't have a lot of experience with them. I started buying cat food and putting it on the back porch with a bowl of water. I bought Friskies in a box for Kitty. He seemed to like that. One time, I bought him some generic-brand food in an effort to save a couple of bucks. When Kitty went to eat it, he acted as though he had put his face in something that smelled terrible. He totally snubbed it. I felt bad and picked up a box of Friskies the next night on my way home from work. He wolfed that down. I put the bag of generic cat food on a shelf in the garage, where the mice eventually got to it.

Even though Kitty was living outdoors, he didn't look skinny and appeared to be well fed. I suspected another neighbor might have been feeding him, in addition to what I gave him, and the birds and mice he was catching in my backyard.

Kitty was a heck of a mouser! On several occasions, I saw him playing with something in the grass. After walking over to investigate, I would discover that he was playing with a mouse or a mole. On one occasion, I actually heard the mouse squealing while Kitty batted it around. I felt bad for the mouse Kitty was torturing, so I shooed Kitty away and put the mouse out of its misery with a shovel and tossed it into the weeds. Sometimes I would find a half-eaten mouse on the back porch.

Kitty was good at catching birds too. One evening, I got home from work and was talking on my cell phone as I pulled into the driveway. As I was finishing up the call, I walked onto the back porch. Out of the corner of my eye, I saw a flock of birds begin to take off from the yard. Out from the weeds jetted Kitty, and he leaped three or four feet into the air and pulled down the last bird to take off. He was clearly stalking these birds but I hadn't seen him. He batted this poor bird back and forth with his front paws, picked it up in his mouth, and brought it up on the porch, where he dropped it. The bird was flopping around, and I said, "Kitty?" Kitty then picked it up and took it into the garage, where he dropped it again. As with the mouse, I shooed Kitty away and put the bird out of its misery.

That summer I did a lot of work outside on the house and the property. I replaced some rotten windowsills and painted the windows, pulled a lot of vines, and cut down sumac trees—stuff like that. Kitty often hung out with me while I was working. He would quietly walk over and lie down on the grass and watch me. Half the time I didn't even know he was there until he decided to walk over and bump up against my leg, or I turned around and happened to see him sitting there. And then I would say, "Kitty!" He was the coolest cat I had ever met. Often, I would just be hanging out on the back porch in the evening, and Kitty would come sauntering along and jump up on my lap and lie down. He wouldn't stay long, but he'd be there long enough to let me know he trusted me and for me to start developing a real fondness for him.

That was also the summer I got married.

• *Chapter 3* •

LOVE AND MARRIAGE

I HAD MET MY FIANCÉE in August of the previous year. She had recently rented the top floor of a house that was across the street from the condo where I was living. One Saturday morning, I was working on one of my motorcycles in the garage when I saw this absolutely stunning woman jogging up the street. I paused to admire her beauty. I had lived there for ten years and thought I knew everyone who lived on the street, but I had never seen this woman before. A few evenings later, I went into the local taproom for a beer, and that same gorgeous woman was sitting at the bar next to an empty stool. Needless to say, I sat down next to her.

We seemed to hit it off right away. It was as if our eyes sparkled as we talked with each other. Not only was I smitten with her, but I could tell she was very interested in me, too. She worked for a company that had recently transferred her to the local office, and that's why she was new to the area. I had only had a couple of beers, but before leaving the bar that evening, I made it a point to get her contact information.

We started e-mailing right away and meeting for lunch or dinner almost immediately. Since she liked motorcycles, I would often pick her up on mine, and we would ride for hours. I saw her almost every day from that point forward. I was falling in love.

I asked her to marry me after only a few months, and she moved into my condo with me a month or two after that. I had never been married before, but I was convinced she was the person I had been waiting for my whole life.

Previously, I had only met two women whom I had had those kinds of feelings for. One of them I had known when I was in college, but I had been too young and immature and hadn't pursued my feelings. I always regretted that.

The other I had known when I was in my early thirties, but I had quickly come to the realization that she was not ready to settle down, although we had had a ton of fun riding motorcycles together and hanging out. I would have asked that woman to marry me if I had thought she had been ready. She was originally from the West Coast and ended up moving back a short time after we met.

My fiancée and I were married in July. We had an absolutely beautiful wedding, with many of our friends and family in attendance. We had it at one of the local inns, where most of our guests got rooms. We had a great weekend! Up to that point, it had been the best weekend of my life.

• *Chapter 4* •

EASY COME, EASY GO

THAT SUMMER WAS THE BEST summer of my life. Not only did I meet Kitty (although I didn't know at the time the impact he would have on me), but I also got married to the woman of my dreams. Unfortunately, things didn't work out the way they were supposed to with my wife. I got home from work on Friday evening, September 22, and she was gone. She had written me a "Dear John" e-mail that morning and set her system to send it at five, when I was to be leaving work. When I got home, I thought it odd that her car wasn't in the driveway, but when I came in the front door and saw many of her belongings gone, I was devastated. I tried to call her on her cell phone, but she didn't answer. I then frantically ran to my computer, and that is when I saw her e-mail.

She said a bunch of stuff about not being a coward, this being the hardest thing she had ever had to do, hoping that I could find it in my heart to forgive her someday, etc. When I read these words now, all I see is blah, blah, blah. But at the time, I was heartbroken.

Over the next couple of months, we continued our relationship under the guise that she would be moving back. She said that she was confused and just needed some time to work things out in her head, or something like that, but that she would be coming home. We would meet for breakfast or dinner, and I was trying to be patient and give her the space she said she needed. She even picked me up from work one evening in a limousine and took me out to a fancy restaurant. This was supposed to be some kind of reward for being patient. When it became apparent that she wasn't moving back, I filed for divorce. I didn't even know where she was living and had to hire an attorney and a private investigator to find out. As it turned out, a former boyfriend of hers had bought a house for her less than a month after she moved out of our home. As I later discovered, she had had an on-and-off relationship with this guy for a couple of years. After we were married, he decided that he still wanted her in his life and made her an offer that I guess she just couldn't refuse—a new house, car, jewelry, and from what I understand, many other things.

We were officially divorced the following spring. To this day, I don't know why she ever married me. I sarcastically tell people who ask me about my marriage that I was married for only ten minutes.

So, within three months, I experienced the best day of

my life and the worst.

• *Chapter 5* •

MOVING INSIDE

THAT FALL, WHEN IT STARTED to get cold out,
Kitty would often try to get in the house, like when I was
bringing in groceries and had the door open. Since he
was full of fleas and ticks, I would simply follow him in,
gently pick him up, and take him back outside. One
Saturday afternoon when I had the basement hatchway
door open while I was doing some work, Kitty snuck in,
curled up on a tarp underneath my workbench, and took
a snooze. I found him when I was cleaning up and
getting ready to close up the basement. As with the
previous times when he had tried to get in, I picked him

up, took him upstairs, and put him down on the grass.

Since he really wanted a place to stay inside, I installed one of those swinging two-way pet doors so that he could sleep in the garage. I put his food and water bowl in a corner, right next to a big pillow for him to lie on. At first, Kitty didn't know what to make of the swinging pet door. I actually had to show him how to use it. But he caught on fast. I held the pet door open and coaxed him to come through. He would be lying on his pillow every morning when I left for work.

One Saturday, I was in the garage getting something off the shelf when Kitty rubbed up against my leg. It startled me at first since I thought I was alone. I said, "Kitty!" He had come through the swinging door, and I hadn't heard him. Whenever he rubbed against me after that, I knew right away it was Kitty, and I always said, "Kitty!" Since I was now living by myself in the house that I was supposed to have been sharing with my wife, having Kitty around and taking care of him helped me to get my mind off of my marital problems.

In late November, when it really started to get cold out, he looked up at me one morning and said with those big, beautiful green eyes, "Dude, come on. It's so cold out here; just let me in." So I told him I would.

That Saturday after getting out of bed, I went downstairs to the garage and locked the swinging pet door so Kitty couldn't get out. After showering and eating breakfast, I took Kitty to Petco for his shots and tests and to get all the fleas and ticks removed. I carried him in a cat carrier I had borrowed from one of my colleagues at work.

Kitty was a long-haired cat, a Maine coon, so during the cold-weather months, his fur would get really bushy. Randy said he would get huge during the winter, when he was living outside. When I first met Kitty earlier that year, he still had much of his winter coat, but it was all matted. Much of it was actually hanging off him, and he would drag it as he walked. I cut off as much of it as I could with plain old scissors while we were hanging out on the porch one evening.

Since the weather had already been below freezing for an extended period of time, the fleas had all died, and they weren't really an issue. But Kitty still had plenty of ticks, so he spent most of the day at the groomer's. He got a flea and tick bath, and they shaved him up really well. They gave him the lion cut, which essentially emphasizes the cat's fur around his head, like a male lion's mane. The groomer also leaves the fur on at the end of the tail and doesn't shave the cat's legs. Everything else is trimmed. Kitty looked like he was wearing boots; he looked so cute!

When I brought Kitty home from Petco, he officially became an indoor cat, something he had been trying to become for months. He slept in bed with me that night.

He was in heaven. I woke up the following morning, and he was lying right next to me, leaning on my back, as I generally sleep on my side. I think he liked the warmth.

Kitty, after coming home from one of his many trips to the groomer

• *Chapter 6* •

FALLING IN LOVE AGAIN

DURING THE COURSE OF THE next several months, Kitty settled in, and we fell into a routine. Even though I knew he had liked living outside, he never once tried to get out of the house. He really liked his new home, and he loved sleeping in bed with his new daddy (how Kitty's future vet would refer to me when talking to him). I would give him Greenies and Temptations treats at night before going to bed. He loved them, and I loved giving them to him. He had a litter box on the first floor in the kitchen, where he also had his food and water bowls. I began feeding him Purina Cat Chow, which he seemed to like just as much as Friskies in a box.

One night while we were watching television before bed, Kitty sneezed, and it prompted me to think I had grown pretty fond of this little guy and would hate it if something happened to him. Kitty had become my best friend. He had actually helped me to get through the bad breakup with my ex-wife (although, as I would eventually discover, I was not fully over that). He was always happy to see me when I got home, often sitting on the stereo next to the back door or in a sunny spot on the floor, waiting for me. He would hang out with me while I made dinner or cleaned dishes in the sink in the evening. If I hadn't fed him yet, he would sometimes nip at my calves, letting me know I needed to feed him before I fed myself, which I always did. (My mother told me Kitty nipped at her ankles in the backyard when she first met him in 2006.)

I would talk to him as I worked. Sometimes I'd even

sing to him. I made up this song that I sang to the tune of "Little Lover" by AC/DC. But I'd sing "Kitty Lover" instead. The song went like this:

Kitty Loverrrr, you're my sexxxxy lover boy.

You're my Kitty Loverrrr, and you're my sexy lover boy.

I would make up a bunch of other verses, usually relevant to what we were doing at the moment or what had gone on that day at work, or I would make some derogatory comment about my ex-wife or someone else from my past. He always rubbed up against my leg when I sang to him.

I made an appointment for him at one of the local vets for a routine checkup. Kitty passed with flying colors; the vet said he was as healthy as a horse. While I still took Kitty, and eventually my other cats, to Petco for routine vaccinations (they cost a third of what they do at the regular vet), this particular vet became Kitty's regular doctor for everything else.

Kitty was a very easy cat to care for. He was low key, healthy, and without any special needs. I could go away on vacation and leave plenty of food and water, and he would be fine, but he really loved to hang out with me. He wasn't a lap cat though. In fact, he didn't even like to be petted too much. A little here and there, but if you petted him too much, he would jump down from the bed or couch and go sit somewhere else. However, he relished being with me, whether it was sitting next to me on the couch, lying next to me in bed, or just being in the same room with me.

Occasionally, Kitty would sit very close to me and put his front paws on me, but he rarely would climb all the way up on my lap. If he did, he wouldn't stay long. I've read that this type of behavior is typical of Maine coons. Kitty did, however, like to have his nose rubbed. With my hand on his head, I'd rub his nose with my thumb, and he would push his little nose up into my thumb. It was so cute. He also liked his butt rubbed at the base of his tail. If he was lying on his stomach and I rubbed his butt, he would push his butt up toward my hand. I've heard people refer to this maneuver as "elevator butt," because my rubbing him would cause his butt to rise.

Kitty and I developed a very close bond through the years. He was my boy, and he was so cool. I loved Kitty so much. And I knew he knew that I loved him, which was important to me. Kitty lived like a king. I took very good care of him, and he brought much joy to my life.

Kitty snoozing in the bedroom in 2008

• *Chapter 7* •

MOVING BACK

EVEN THOUGH MY EX-WIFE and I were divorced, she was still trying to get back together with me. Based on what she had already done to me, I had my doubts. She was living out of state near her family, but she told me that she wanted to move back. We were still e-mailing, and we would occasionally talk on the telephone. Sometimes we even met in person, mostly when she was in the area for work. I was still in love with her but didn't quite know what to make of her offer. I told her that she wasn't going to move back in with me but that it was a free country, and she could move to wherever else she wanted. I agreed to begin seeing her again if she did move back to the area. She ended up moving in early 2008 to an apartment about seven or eight miles from where I lived, and we started dating again.

I know what you're thinking: Why the heck would you want to start seeing your ex-wife again? She is an ex for a reason. Well, I guess I had some unfinished business. She was the woman whom I had been waiting for my whole life. She was the one I wanted to be with. When we were together, it seemed as if everything was all right with the world. I had history with this woman, even though some of it had caused me great emotional pain. If there was a possibility of working things out with her, then I wanted to try. I knew it would take time for her to earn my trust again and wanted to give her the opportunity to do so. I wanted things to be like they were when we first met. Since I was still relatively new to the area, I had few close friends who lived nearby. Most of the people I knew were simply acquaintances. I was lonely, and I was vulnerable. In retrospect, I was out of my mind, but at the time, it seemed like the right thing to do. I thought that if we could successfully "date" for five years, then maybe she could move back in with me and Kitty. We had gotten married too quickly and hadn't had a proper courtship to begin with.

• *Chapter 8* •

INTRODUCING SQUEAKERS

TAKING CARE OF KITTY HAD caused me to develop a real soft spot in my heart for abandoned cats. In the fall of 2009, I rescued another cat I named Squeakers because he squeaked when you picked him up. Squeakers had been living under a porch at my ex-wife's apartment complex when I first met him. I had heard him crying and had seen him a few times over the course of about three weeks. He was friendly but scared. He had clearly been abandoned. A couple of times I saw him standing in front of an apartment door, crying, like he was asking to be let in. Unfortunately, there are too many irresponsible pet owners who abandon their cats when they move, and that is what I suspect happened to Squeakers.

At first, Squeakers lived in the basement until I could get him his shots and tests and take him to the groomer to get cleaned up. After this had been done and his test results came back negative, Squeakers moved upstairs with Kitty and me.

Kitty didn't want to have anything to do with him. Heck, he was used to being the only cat, and he liked it that way. He would hiss at Squeakers and torment him. I would come home from work, and Squeaks, which I call him for short, would be nowhere to be found. I quickly learned that his hiding place was behind the couch in the living room.

A couple of times during the evening when I was in the kitchen, Kitty would be chasing Squeaks or something, and they would really get into it. Kitty would be hissing and clawing at Squeakers. That would lead to a decision to give Kitty a time-out, and I put him in the bathroom and closed the door. I kept him in there for probably five minutes. Kitty weighed eighteen pounds, whereas Squeakers was only about ten pounds. Kitty could have demolished him if he had wanted to, and I didn't want that to happen.

Fortunately, this only lasted for two or three weeks. Kitty and Squeakers ended up becoming good buddies. They hung out all the time. The first time I saw Kitty actually grooming Squeakers, it warmed my heart. He was licking the top of Squeakers' head, and Squeaks just stood there and let him. He was no longer scared of Kitty.

They became such good pals that Kitty used to let Squeakers torment him. When Squeakers was feeling playful, he would bat Kitty and try to wrestle with him. Kitty was kind of indifferent, as if to say, "Dude, leave me alone. I just wanna hang out." But Squeakers would insist that they wrestle. So Kitty would get up and wrestle with Squeakers, flip him over on his back (again, Kitty was almost twice the size of Squeakers), and Squeakers would get up and run into the other room. A moment later, he would run back to Kitty and try to get him to wrestle again. Kitty would flip Squeakers over on his back again, Squeaks would get up and run away, and then he'd come back a moment later for some more. It was actually funny to watch. Seeing them play like that brought a smile to my face.

Kitty and Squeakers hanging out on the couch in 2010

Even though Squeakers is a domestic shorthair, he shed more than Kitty, especially in the spring. I got into the habit of brushing him most evenings before bed. At that point, Kitty hadn't really warmed to brushing, but I think Squeakers must have had someone in his life who brushed him, because he loved it. Since Kitty was a longhaired cat, it could be argued that he could've used a brushing just as much as Squeaks. Kitty would often sit on the kitchen floor and watch me brush Squeakers, and he would see how much Squeaks enjoyed it.

Well, one night Kitty got up to come over and see what this brushing stuff was all about, and I brushed him too. Each night I would brush Kitty a little more than the previous night. He seemed to like it—maybe not as much as Squeakers did, but I could tell that he thought the brush felt good, especially on his butt.

Kitty grooming Squeakers in the kitchen in 2010

• *Chapter 9* •

GIRLENE JOINS THE FAMILY

ONE DAY THAT SAME YEAR, I was cutting the grass when a feral cat crawled into my garage and had three kittens. Unfortunately, the mother cat, whom I named Kitty Momma, had passed along some disease to her kittens, and two of them didn't make it. The surviving kitten was hospitalized twice, but we were able to nurse her back to health. I named her Samantha, but I called her my Little Girl, which morphed into Girlie, which morphed into Girlene. Girlene is Irish for "little girl" (although I've also seen it spelled "Girleen"). The vet knows her as Samantha, but this little girl recognizes her name as Girlene.

So we added another member to the Kitty family. While Kitty was initially reluctant to let Squeakers join, he didn't pay Girlene any mind. I'm not sure if it was because she was so young or because she was a female, or maybe it was a combination of both. But nonetheless, we had one happy family. Everyone got along and hung out together, and everyone respected one another's bowls at dinnertime, which I've come to learn is huge for a happy kitty family.

Kitty, Squeakers, and Girlene hanging out in the kitchen in 2010

Since Kitty Momma was a feral cat, there was no hope for her ever becoming a pet and living peacefully with me and my other cats. Whenever I went into the garage to feed her, she would hiss at me and back into a corner. All she wanted was to be let out of the garage, so I borrowed a Havahart trap and took her to the vet one morning before work to get spayed. I picked her up that night on my way home. The vet suggested keeping her in the garage for a few days so she could heal, which I did.

That weekend, I decided it was time to give Kitty Momma her freedom and opened the garage door. I expected that she would run out and I'd never see her again, but she hid under a cabinet instead. An hour or so later, I checked on her, and she was gone. I occasionally would see her in the backyard and started putting cat food on the back porch, as I had done when I first met Kitty. I stopped seeing her periodically about a year and a half later.

• *Chapter 10* •

HERE COMES GYPSY

IN THE FALL OF 2011, I rescued another cat. Yeah, I know what you're thinking: Another one?

I had seen this guy, whom I eventually named Gypsy, eating out of a Dumpster at my ex-wife's apartment complex. He was really friendly too. He always trilled when he saw me and had a really nice personality. So I figured, "What's one more?"

I brought Gypsy home and put him in the basement, as I had done with Squeaks. I got him his shots and tests and a shave at the groomer's. He was skinny, but he fattened up in about two weeks once he had unlimited access to "crunchies"—what I call hard cat food. I also gave him canned food in the evenings. Unfortunately, Gypsy had a particularly bad case of fleas, and it took several months to get rid of them. I had to give all four of my cats a medication called Revolution for three months. Once we got rid of the fleas, Gypsy came upstairs to live with the rest of us.

Kitty and Gypsy did not hit it off at all! Gypsy is a Maine coon like Kitty, but he's two or three pounds smaller and can be pretty naughty. He's my only cat that'll stick his head in the trash can to see what's available, a bad habit he developed when he was living outside and eating from Dumpsters. He's also my only cat that plays with and chases his tail. I often tell him he's going to go blind if he keeps doing that, but he continues to anyway.

While at first I discouraged Kitty from messing with Gypsy, I actually noticed that Gypsy would behave himself when he was around Kitty. So whenever they got into it, I let it go. While Gypsy can still be very naughty, he's not as bad as he was when I first brought him upstairs. I partially attribute that to Kitty helping me train him. While they never became good friends, Gypsy did respect Kitty and would tread lightly whenever Kitty was present. As a matter of fact, sometimes when Kitty was around, Gypsy would drop to the floor and stay down. This, of course, was Gypsy's way of letting Kitty know he understood Kitty had alpha-kitty status. Not only was Kitty the alpha, but he also became the enforcer and would not allow Gypsy to mess with Squeakers or Girlene, either.

One Saturday afternoon that winter, I was painting in my upstairs hallway. I turned my back for literally five seconds, and I heard a kitty scuffle. Kitty and Gypsy had gotten into it. Well, I looked around the corner, and paint was splashed all over the upstairs hallway, and Kitty was sitting there covered in paint. I went to grab him, and he ran down the stairs, tracking paint as he went. I followed, picked him up, put him in the bathroom, and closed the door so he wouldn't get paint everywhere. I was using shellac-based paint that had to be cleaned with ammonia. I grabbed the ammonia from the kitchen and a wad of paper towels and went in the bathroom to start trying to clean Kitty with the ammonia-saturated paper towels, when a lightbulb went on above my head—ding. Rubbing ammonia on Kitty was a bad idea. So I called Petco and found out its grooming salon was still open. I told the person on the phone that I had an emergency situation and was told I could bring Kitty in.

After dropping Kitty off, I went back home and cleaned up all the paint. What a fiasco! I picked up Kitty a couple of hours later, and he had been cleaned up really well and shaved, too. That was the last time I painted anything without locking my cats in the bedroom first.

Unfortunately, Gypsy had some health problems, and I had to start feeding him prescription food. This meant he had to be confined to a bedroom at mealtime (so he wouldn't eat the other cats' food, and they couldn't eat his). Since I was trying to fatten up my skinny boy, Squeakers, by giving him unlimited access to crunchies during the day while I was at work, I had to keep Gypsy in the bedroom most of the day. As a result, he and Kitty never had the full opportunity to work out their issues. But at night, we would all sleep in bed together: me and four kitties! I used to thank Kitty every day for letting me bring home all these other cats.

Kitty, Gypsy, and Squeakers enjoying the view of the
backyard and the warm weather in 2012

• *Chapter 11* •

UNFINISHED BUSINESS FINISHED

AFTER MY EX-WIFE HAD moved back to the area, we began regularly seeing each other again, but we were never able to re-create what we had had before she left. While I had provided her with the opportunity to earn my trust back, the truth was that I was never going to trust her again. I mean, I could trust her to meet me for dinner at a certain time, but I was never going to develop that deep-down trust in her ever again—the kind of trust you reserve for only the most important people in your life, the kind of trust you reserve for family and your closest friends, the kind of trust that is shared between significant others. The pain that I had experienced was just too great. Our breakup was long and drawn out, and I realize now that we should have never been together, but I would never have met Kitty if we hadn't.

During these on-and-off periods I had with my ex-wife, Kitty was always there for me. The relationship I had with him was always on. He loved me unconditionally, as I loved him. I slowly came to realize that the relationship I had expected to have with my ex-wife I had developed with Kitty. I shared my home with him, along with our other rescued felines. This might sound funny, how a relationship with a cat could replace a relationship with a person, but it did. I had plenty of relationships with people in my life, and I had plenty of room for other relationships. I had built this kitty family of abandoned and sick cats, and I had come to realize that it replaced what I had expected to have with my ex-wife. So when that relationship ended in the summer of

2012, a year short of my self-imposed five-year time frame, I really wasn't that choked up. In fact, I was completely indifferent. She had lost her job a year earlier and hadn't been able to find another, and said she wanted to move to another state. I owned a house and had a good job, and I wasn't going to move.

I had slowly fallen out of love with her, and the unfinished business was now finished.

• *Chapter 12* •

KITTY GETS SICK

IN LATE AUGUST 2014, I noticed Kitty had been scratching his ears and had a few scabs on them. The last few times I had petted him, he had felt like maybe he was losing some weight as well. I thought this was a good time to take him to the vet for a checkup. I made an appointment and took him in one night after work. The vet said he simply had an ear infection and gave me some ointment to clear it up. She also said one of his lymph nodes felt enlarged. She thought his system was probably just fighting something off (kind of like when we get colds and the lymph nodes in our neck get sore)

and that it was most likely no big deal. She suggested bringing him back in a month for a follow-up visit.

I brought Kitty back to the vet a month later, and she said that not only was that one lymph node bigger, but the others were swollen too. She suggested doing a blood workup and taking some x-rays. While she was able to take the blood that evening, she said the x-rays would have to be conducted the following morning and that Kitty could spend the night. I told her Kitty was going home with me and I would bring him in the following day before work.

The next morning after getting ready for work, I couldn't find Kitty. I was calling for him and searching every room, and I was getting concerned since I knew he might be sick. I spent around twenty minutes looking for him; I checked all the usual hiding places, with no luck. I've read that when cats don't feel well they often curl up somewhere and hide until they feel better. I've also read that they do this when they are preparing to die. I went through every room, inch by inch, calling for him, even taking apart beds with the thought that maybe he had crawled up into one of the box springs. As I finished checking a room, I would close the door so he couldn't sneak in there when I went to another room.

Well, I went through every room and still couldn't find him. As I opened the door and came out of my bedroom, Kitty was sitting there in the hall. He looked at me as if to say, "Dude, you've been calling my name for the last twenty minutes. What do you want? I'm trying to sleep." I scooped him up and put him in the cat carrier. To this day, I still don't know where he was hiding.

I dropped Kitty off at the vet and then left work early to pick him up. When the vet showed me Kitty's x-rays, she said it looked like he had a mass in his chest cavity and another in his abdomen. She said her guess was that it was lymphoma, but we would have to do a biopsy to be sure. She also said a few other tests would be needed. She said if it was lymphoma, she could refer me to a pet oncologist. I didn't know what to think or say. I was stunned, but I tried to keep my cool and approach it as I do other issues in my life, by getting additional information and working to solve the problem.

I talked with her about all the possible options and costs. She said that treating lymphoma in a cat usually costs in the range of $6,000 to $8,000, but realistically, it tended to cost much more. She also reminded me that, at that stage, the cancer couldn't necessarily be cured, but rather postponed, and that Kitty would eventually die.

So I had a decision to make. I took Kitty home and put him in one of my spare bedrooms, the one I call the Blue Room, so that the other cats wouldn't mess with him. It was a Friday evening, and my girlfriend, Carrie, whom I had met in the summer of 2013, and I had plans to go out. We went to my friend Megan's bar for a couple of drinks. As it turned out, I really wasn't in the mood to sit at the bar, and Megan had taken the night off anyway, so after one drink, we left to go home. I spent most of the weekend hanging with Kitty and all of the weekend thinking about his problem.

I thought about how old Kitty was. I had known him for nine years, and Randy said he had been living in the backyard for two or three years, and he had obviously been someone's pet before that. So I guessed he was at least fourteen or fifteen years old. Kitty had had a nice, long life. He had lived like a king, and I didn't have an extra six or eight grand. Most importantly, I didn't want to put Kitty through biopsies, chemotherapy, or radiation treatment. So after struggling with the decision all weekend, I made up my mind to simply make the remainder of his life as comfortable as I could.

I slept with him in the Blue Room every night and fed him canned food for every meal. I also made certain he had an unlimited amount of crunchies, and I cleaned his litter box twice a day. I gave him as many Greenies and Temptations treats as he could eat at night before bed. I usually would visit my family for the Thanksgiving and Christmas holidays, but in 2014 I stayed home and took care of Kitty. My Christmas card that year featured a picture of Kitty and me kissing, with the caption: "Here's to Kitty, who rescued his Daddy after his Daddy rescued him." My sister had given me the idea for that when she said in a text message after learning of Kitty's diagnosis that he had been very lucky to have me, as I had been very lucky to have him. She suggested that the quality of his life had increased tenfold the day he met me. He had helped me to get through the bad breakup with my ex-wife. He had become my best friend. He loved me unconditionally and showed me every day.

My 2014 Christmas card picture that had this caption:
"Here's to Kitty, who rescued his Daddy after his Daddy
rescued him."

In early November, Kitty had another appointment at
the vet so she could see how he was doing. She
confirmed that he was hanging in there but said that
things could change very quickly. She said it could be as
little as two weeks or as long as three months, but she
didn't think it would be much longer than that.

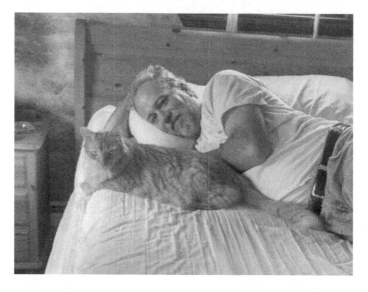

Kitty and his daddy hanging out in the Blue Room

Over the course of the next couple of months, the lymph node under Kitty's left ear became very large. I tried not to touch it when I petted his head, as I thought it might be sore for him. His appetite also started to go downhill. I had to change his food every couple of weeks to get him to eat, and I had to sit with him and talk to him to encourage him to do so. I would sing the "Kitty Lover" song, tell him he was a good boy—stuff like that.

He would eat a little and then walk away, and I would pick up his bowl and put it down in front of him, and he would eat a little more. I had always given him Friskies canned food. He soured on it at some point in November or December. I tried two different flavors of Friskies Senior Diet, which he liked at first, but that only lasted a couple of weeks. So I bought a bunch of cans of Albacore tuna, which he liked at first. I bought different flavors of Fancy Feast, Sheba, and others I can't even remember. I also tried Bumble Bee Chunk Light Tuna. At first he liked all of these, but eventually he would sour on them.

• *Chapter 13* •

KITTY'S LAST FEW DAYS

ON MONDAY, FEBRUARY 23, Kitty had an appointment at the vet. It had been three months since his last visit. He was down to thirteen pounds, but that was only a pound lighter than three months earlier. The vet said his lungs and heart both sounded fine and that his abdomen felt good. She actually thought Kitty was doing very well, under the circumstances. That made me feel good. I shared with her how I was changing his food and how I had to coax him to eat. She suggested Kitty could last another six to eight months! She also said that in rare cases, cats live two or three years after being diagnosed with this illness. That was encouraging.

That Saturday morning, Kitty didn't eat his breakfast—a couple of licks, but that's about it. While I was a little concerned, he had done this before, and always in a day or so he would go back to eating his food, or most of it. That Saturday night, he got an early dinner, but he ate the same as he had in the morning: a few licks, and that was it. He then jumped off the bed and went to lie behind the armoire. Even though the room was fully carpeted, a month or two earlier I had pulled the armoire away from the wall and put a towel back there for him. He liked to lie either behind it or next to it. I went downstairs and got him a few tablespoons of a different cat food, but he wasn't interested in that either. I even tried the smelly tuna with no luck. That night I slept on the floor with him for a few hours. We fell asleep with me gently petting him and telling him he was a good boy.

The following morning was the same: he wouldn't eat. I was lying on the floor with him, just watching him. It seemed as though his breaths were shorter and faster, too, which concerned me. But he seemed to be comfortable just lying on the carpet or on the towel. That day I spent several hours with him in the bedroom. I actually picked him up and put him on the bed, where we lay together. That night was the same thing with the food—he just wasn't interested in eating. I slept on the floor with him all night. I lay there and could hear him breathing. I woke up at one point because I had to use the bathroom, and he was lying next to me, actually leaning on my back like that first time he had slept on the bed with me back in 2006. Monday morning was the same with the food: a couple of licks, even though I tried two different kinds. His breathing was the same too.

I was obviously very concerned. After getting to work that morning, I called the vet and talked with Kelly, the vet's assistant. I told her Kitty was not doing well and shared my observations with her. I said I planned to check on him during my lunch hour to see how he was doing. I told her that even though he had been in a week earlier, I might need to bring him in that day. She said I could bring him in at two or two thirty in the afternoon if I wanted to. I said I would give her a call and let her know.

I left work at one in the hopes that I would be back in an hour, but I told my coworkers I might not be. I turned off my computer and took my backpack with me just in case.

I got home, and Kitty was lying next to the armoire on the carpet. I tried to get him to eat, with no luck. I lay on the floor next to him for about forty-five minutes. His breathing was not good. I went into the other room to observe Squeakers' breathing. His breaths were long and slow, whereas Kitty's were short and fast. Kitty's whole body seemed to be struggling to get air. His nostrils would flare with each breath. I lay there petting him and asked him several times what he wanted me to do. He would simply lay his head back down on the carpet, as though he was telling me he just wanted to sleep. This was when I realized I had to let Kitty go. I called Kelly and told her I was bringing him in.

Kitty was very calm on the ride over to the vet. He lay in his cat carrier next to me, and I talked to him as we drove. Through the years, Kitty had become used to taking periodic drives to the vet or the groomer. But in the early days, he didn't like it. He would meow most of the way, and he would sometimes pant, which meant he was very stressed.

I had been preparing for this for months, but it still sucked. As I walked into the vet's office with Kitty, I told Kelly this might be Kitty's last trip to the vet. She brought us back to the examining room right away, and I took Kitty out of the carrier. I held him on my lap while we waited for the vet to arrive. Kitty was kind of restless and jumped off my lap and went under the chair. I picked him up and put him back in the cat carrier, where I knew he would be more comfortable. While it was sometimes a chore to get him in the carrier at home, especially in the early years, he would voluntarily get into the carrier at the vet's office because he knew that he would be going home.

The vet came into the examining room and took a look at Kitty. She said she didn't hear any fluid in his lungs, but there was obviously something pressing on either his lungs or his airway that was causing him difficulty. She also said he had developed what she called a galloping heartbeat. Instead of a steady bump-bump, bump-bump, she said it sounded like bump-gurgle, bump-gurgle, like with the rhythm and speed of a galloping horse. It hadn't been doing that when we were in a week earlier. She said they could pump him up with steroids to reduce the internal swelling, but in three or four days we would probably be back to where we were at that moment. She said she only made that suggestion in case I felt like I needed a few extra days with him.

Kitty had had a great life. He had lived like a king. He was well fed, always had a clean litter box, had a very comfortable home with many great places to sleep, and had a daddy who cared for him very much. While I knew this was a battle we weren't going to win, Kitty and I sure had fought the good fight! When we had been in the vet's office the previous week, she said he had done much better than she had expected. But now it was time to say good-bye to Kitty. When he and I had been lying on the floor in the Blue Room earlier that afternoon, one of the things I had considered was that I could just let him die peacefully at home. But my fear was that I would be at work or something and he would suffer for his last hours, and I didn't want that to happen. That would not be peaceful. I didn't want Kitty to suffer. So I gave the vet the go-ahead to do what she needed to do.

Kelly and the vet took Kitty into the back room to get him prepped, which involved shaving his leg and putting an IV catheter into it. They brought Kitty back a few minutes later. When they opened the door to bring him in, I noticed that his pupils were very large; he knew something was going on. But they seemed to get smaller when he saw me. They had him wrapped in a towel and laid him on the examining table.

The vet shared with me some information about involuntary muscle movements—that after he passed, his body could continue to twitch—and I said I understood. She gave Kitty a shot of saline to clear the IV and then told me to let her know when I was ready. I had my hand on Kitty's back and began to sing the "Kitty Lover" song. I gave her a nod, and she put her hand under Kitty's chin and gently laid his head down. I respected her for that. She had obviously done this before and knew what to expect, whereas I had no idea. I petted Kitty a couple of more times, then got up, put the chair I had been sitting on back in the corner, grabbed the cat carrier, and said, "I gotta go." I was sobbing. I cried in the truck the whole way home. I have had other sad days in my life, but that was the saddest.

When I got home, my other cats didn't greet me at the back door like they usually do when I get in from work. It was too early in the afternoon. I went upstairs, and they were in the back bedroom sleeping. I picked up Girlene and sat down on the futon. Usually when I hold Girlene like that, she'll start purring. She didn't; I think it was because I was crying. But she didn't get off me cithcr. In fact, it seemed like she was hugging me. I sat there for about ten minutes, and she lay on my chest the entire time. She and Squeakers slept very close to their daddy that night.

The following morning, I went into the office, and there was a card sitting in front of my computer. I had texted my colleague Sheryl about Kitty the previous afternoon. She and two of my other colleagues had signed it. After reading it, I sat there and silently cried for about twenty minutes. I put my hands over my face so my coworkers wouldn't hear me, but they knew I was crying. I was so sad. I care more about my cats than I do about most people. Kitty was my boy! He had always been there for me. Whereas others in my life had screwed with my emotions, I had always been able to count on Kitty to greet me at the back door when I got home, or rub up against my leg when he came walking into the room and saw me, or just sit on the couch and watch a movie with me. I could always count on his loyalty. While I knew that Kitty knew I loved him, I also knew he loved me too.

Kitty had such an impact on my life, more so than most people do. He taught me about what is most important in life—not cars or motorcycles or jobs, but relationships. He taught me unconditional love. He had been there for me during one of my most difficult times and had helped me to survive the emotional pain of my divorce. It was almost as if he knew that I was now with Carrie, and that I was going to be fine. He had fulfilled his mission. I truly believe Kitty and I had met for a reason. I had taken care of him, and he had taken care of me. He will forever be a part of my life.

Kitty lying with his daddy in bed on February 19, 2015, eleven days before his last visit to the vet

ABOUT THE AUTHOR

Shawn Flynn spent over twenty-five years in a market-research career before he stepped away to pursue his passion for writing. He knew he wanted to explore his deep connection with cats, particularly the first cat he ever rescued.

Flynn and his girlfriend, Carrie, live in Enfield, Connecticut, where he takes care of several indoor and outdoor cats. He also volunteers with several cat rescue groups including the Enfield Community Cat Project.

Reach out to Flynn at shawnpflynn@yahoo.com.

Scan the following codes with the QR Reader on
your smartphone or tablet.

To get the latest on Shawn and all his feline friends,
visit him on Facebook
@ShawnFlynn

OR
@ShawnFlynn.Author

Rate and Review THE KITTY on amazon.com

Rate and Review THE KITTY on goodreads.com

30323072R00057

Made in the USA
Columbia, SC
29 October 2018